All thunderstorms have thunder and lightning. Lightning is the light that we see in the sky. Sometimes it looks like a flash, and sometimes it looks like a line, called a bolt. Lightning is a form of electric current.

a bolt of lightning

Thunder is the sound made by lightning. It can be a low rumble or a sudden loud clap.

Thunderstorms form in big, tall storm clouds called cumulonimbus (/cuemueloanimbus) clouds. Often, these clouds are shaped like a blacksmith's anvil, with a wide, flat top.

an anvil

a storm cloud

Storm clouds often form in tropical parts of the planet, where the weather is hot and wet.

Inside the storm cloud, small cloud droplets rub together with soft hail. This makes static electricity (/elec**tri**sətee/). This is similar to the sort of static you make when you rub a balloon on your head.

The static builds up and up inside the cloud until a lightning bolt shoots out from the bottom of the cloud.

Lightning can go from cloud to ground, from ground to cloud, or from cloud to cloud.

cloud to ground

ground to cloud

cloud to cloud

Thunder and lightning are more common than you might think. There are around 44 lightning strikes somewhere on the planet every second.

Lake Maracaibo (/Mara**cie**boʊ/) in South America has more thunderstorms than anywhere else. There is a thunderstorm there every two or three nights.

Lake Maracaibo

It might look quiet in this picture, but this lake can have thousands of lightning strikes in one night!

Thunderstorms can be caused by some unexpected things.

Helicopters can trigger thunderstorms if they fly into hail, or go too close to the bottom of a storm cloud.

The heat and smoke from forest fires can trigger storms, too.

Believe it or not, hot summer weather causes thunderstorms, as well.

Volcanic ash and gases can cause lightning strikes.

Golf clubs might not cause lightning strikes, but they can attract them — so remember never to play golf in a thunderstorm!

Lightning can be deadly. Tall trees and buildings can attract lightning.

If lightning hits a tree, the sap inside it boils, and the tree can explode. This can make bark fly off the tree, which is why you should never shelter under trees in a thunderstorm.

burnt tree bark

If a tall building is hit by lightning, it can catch fire. To stop this happening, many tall buildings have a lightning rod.

A lightning rod is a metal rod attached to the roof of a tall building. The rod is attached to a long metal wire that goes down to the ground. The lightning hits the lightning rod, and travels safely down the wire and into the ground without harming the building.

There are different sorts of lightning.

Common sorts of lightning are...

**Sheet lightning**, which looks like a cloud of light spread out across the sky.

**Forked lightning**, which splits into lots of lines called forks.

**Streak lightning**, which looks like one bright line going down to the ground.

Less common sorts of lightning are...

**Ribbon lightning**, which looks like ribbons of light. We get ribbon lightning when the wind is very strong.

**Rocket lightning**, which is very slow lightning. It looks like a rocket travelling across the sky.

**Chain (or bead) lightning**, which looks like a string of beads.

**Red sprites**, which are sometimes seen over the top of the storm cloud.

## How far away is a thunderstorm?

If you count slowly between the lightning flash and the thunder, it will tell you how many miles away the thunderstorm is from you.

If you can count to five between the lightning and the thunder, then the storm is one mile away. (One slow count is about the same as one second.)

| Time between lightning and thunder | Miles away |
|---|---|
| 5 seconds | 1 |
| 10 seconds | 2 |
| 15 seconds | 3 |
| 20 seconds | 4 |
| 25 seconds | 5 |

Lightning bolts travel at very high speeds.

If a lightning bolt could travel from the Earth to the Moon, it would take less than an hour to complete the journey!

As lightning can light up the whole sky, you might be surprised to learn that lightning bolts are extremely narrow. They are just 2 or 3cm wide, which is about the same width as an adult's thumb.

same width

Lightning bolts can, however, be very long. Often they are 2 or 3 miles long, but sometimes they can be hundreds of miles long.

Lightning strikes can heat up the sky around them to about five times hotter than the outer layer of the sun.

That is exceedingly hot!

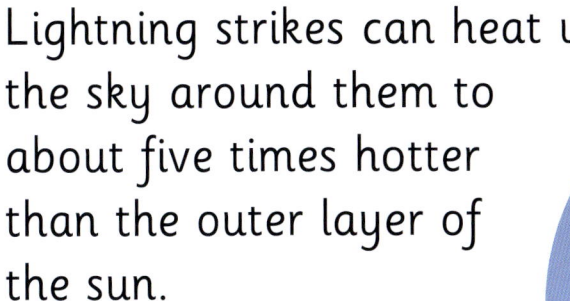

## How to stay safe in a thunderstorm

1. **Do** get into a car or a building if you can.

2. **Do not** carry a metal pole, a golf club or an umbrella.

3. **Do not** swim. Get out of the pool or sea.

4. **Do not** stand on top of a hill. Lie as close to the ground as you can.

5. **Do not** hide under trees.